03036

D0307158

Fal

DAYS THAT CHANGED THE WORLD

THE FALL OF THE
BERLIN WALL

Jeremy Smith

Copyright © ticktock Entertainment Ltd 2003
First published in Great Britain in 2003 by ticktock Media Ltd.,
Unit 2, Orchard Business Centre, North Farm Road, Tunbridge Wells, Kent, TN2 3XF
ISBN 1 86007 422 7 pbk
ISBN 1 86007 429 4 hbk
Printed in Taiwan
A CIP catalogue record for this book is available from the British Library.

CONTENTS

INTRODUCTION *4–7*

BEFORE *a battle of ideologies* *8–15*

FEELINGS OF CHANGE *1960s and 1970s* *16–21*

THE CRITICAL MOMENT *the day the wall fell* *22–29*

AFTERMATH *first contacts* *30–35*

LATER *Germany in the early 1990s* *36–39*

FUTURE *looking forward* *40–41*

TIMELINE *42–43*

GLOSSARY *44–45*

INDEX *46–47*

ACKNOWLEDGEMENTS *48*

INTRODUCTION

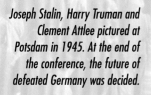

Joseph Stalin, Harry Truman and Clement Attlee pictured at Potsdam in 1945. At the end of the conference, the future of defeated Germany was decided.

On the evening of November 9th, 1989, the concrete wall that had cut Berlin in two for over 30 years was brought crashing down by the people of Berlin themselves. This formidable structure that had wound its way 160 kilometres around the capital of old Germany was dismantled, at first brick-by-brick, then section-by-section, as 'people power' overcame the political divide of East and West.

Checkpoint Charlie in Berlin was one of the few points along the Wall where people could pass from one half of the city to the other – if they had the correct authority.

The reasons behind the building of the Berlin Wall date back over 50 years, to the aftermath of World War II.

After the defeat of Hitler's forces, Germany was divided up between the victorious Allies. The three Western powers – Britain, France and the USA – merged their sectors into one zone, later renamed the FRG (Federal Republic of Germany). The USSR renamed its zone the GDR (German Democratic Republic). However, old

Germany's historic capital, Berlin, remained a problem. Situated over 128 kilometres into Soviet East Germany, Berlin was split into two like the rest of Germany, with West Berlin run along capitalist lines, in stark contrast to the communist East of the city.

Despite this agreement, however, the presence of capitalist and prosperous West Berlin became an increasing problem for the USSR. Although a barrier had been put up between East and West Germany in 1952, East Berlin was still losing thousands of its

Security forces struggled to control crowds on the evening the Wall came down.

citizens every year through West Berlin. People would simply cross over from the other side of the city, re-register as West German citizens and then escape to the West. On the night of August 13th, 1961, the Berlin Wall was put up in an attempt to stem the tide by worried communist authorities. Initially a barbed wire ring through the city, it was soon replaced by a solid concrete barrier that split families apart for decades.

• Berlin

East Germany

West Germany

A map showing the division of Germany, and the location of Berlin deep in the heart of communist East Germany.

The election of Mikhail Gorbachev as the leader of the USSR in the 1980s heralded a period of change which would eventually lead to the dissolution of the USSR.

Over a period of nearly 40 years, hundreds of East Germans lost their lives trying to vault, dig under or smash through the monstrous wall when they were gunned down by border guards. However, growing resentment on both sides of the divide together with thawing relations between the United States and USSR and the election of younger, reformist leaders such as Mikhail Gorbachev in the USSR, the future of the Wall seemed less certain. The worsening economic situation in East Germany also forced its leaders to make human-rights concessions in return for economic aid. Amongst other things, East German leader Eric Honecker suspended the 'shoot-to-kill' policy at the Wall when important state visits took place to avoid acute embarrassment.

By the late 1980s, communist Europe began to fall in on itself. Hungary had dismantled its border with Austria, offering East Germans another escape route into the West. Then in June 1989, the Polish head-of-state, General Jaruzelski, was forced to lift the ban on the workers' union Solidarity and call free elections. In Poland's first poll for over 30 years, Solidarity stormed to victory, with Tadeusz Mazowiecki elected as head of

Eastern Europe's first non-communist government. East Germans started to flood out of the country through foreign embassies, and the pressure was building on the East German authorities to make a change. The Wall seemed somehow less frightening than it had before and by 1989, the people of Berlin were ready to challenge its legitimacy.

After the Wall fell, the political landscape of Europe continued to change. Czechoslovakia, Romania and Hungary ousted their communist governments from power. Then at midnight on October 3rd, 1990, Germany was reunited. A year later, the communist government in the USSR disbanded, bringing an end to the Cold War and the divisions of East and West.

In the 1990s, Germany's new parliament opened – an impressive building with a glass ceiling that aimed to reflect the new transparency of the nation's political system.

Over ten years later, it is clear that reunification has brought problems as well as benefits to the German people, with people in the east of the country still much poorer than those in the west – but the nation has begun to make its mark both in Europe and the world. Germany is one of the strongest supporters of the single European currency, the euro, and has also played a role in military operations in Kosovo and Afghanistan. Whatever the future holds after the fall of the Berlin Wall, the reunited Germany has remained optimistic about what lies ahead.

Jubilant Berliners climbed on top of the Wall to celebrate when they heard that it was to be demolished

To find out why the Berlin Wall was put up, you have to go right back to the beginning of the 20th century. In 1917, the establishment of the world's first communist government in Russia led to increasingly strained relations with the capitalist West. This tension became evident as the victorious Allies sat down to decide how to deal with Germany after World War II. Negotiations ended in an agreement that divided Germany and its capital into East and West. However, when people started to pour out of East Germany into the more prosperous West, the communist authorities decided thast action had to be taken. The answer was the Berlin Wall.

The German Karl Marx was responsible for developing the ideology of communism, together with Friedrich Engels.

Capitalism

Capitalism emphasizes the importance of individual rights, and the power of every person to rise by his or her own efforts and merits. Instead of believing that everyone is equal, capitalism creates opportunities for financial reward to individuals who can develop ideas for making money. Most western economies are based on capitalism.

Communism

By the early 20th century, a new ideology called communism was thriving throughout parts of Europe. It was based on a pamphlet called *The Communist Manifesto*, written by Germans Karl Marx and Friedrich Engels and published in 1847. In it, Marx and Engels attacked capitalism, believing that it created divisions among the people. Instead, they put forward a new philosophy which they said would create a society where everyone was equal. In a communist society, all possessions would be held by the state, and everybody would share equally in the nation's wealth.

The Russian Revolution

Communism had a strong appeal in countries such as Russia, where the rich hoarded incredible wealth and the poor struggled to feed themselves. In 1917, the Russian royal family were ousted by a group of revolutionary communists. Led by Vladimir Lenin, they brutally killed the Czar and his family, and declared a republic — the USSR. It was the world's first communist state. When Lenin was replaced by the more aggressive Joseph Stalin in

STALIN'S empire

Stalin established an iron grip on the USSR through the use of systematic terror. Between 1934 and 1938, a massive purge known as the 'Red Terror' resulted in the the disappearance and death of about three million Russians. Millions of other Russians were taken to work in labour camps, which were known as 'gulags'.

A FRUSTRATED *Germany*

One of the chief causes of World War I and the rise of Hitler was Germany's desire to expand its territory. Envious of the money Britain had made from its empire, Germany embarked on an ambitious navy-building programme. Although Germany's efforts to take European territory were defeated in World War I, its desire remained unquenched, and surfaced again with Hitler's return to power in the 1930s. This time Hitler wanted to unite the German-speaking people of the world under one 'fatherland'. But eventually Hitler's ambitions went way beyond this aim and his troops invaded countries which had never had any connection to Germany.

Great cities such as New York (right) and London have thrived thanks to the philosophy of capitalism.

abolished all other political parties, expanded his own power and introduced a series of racist laws against the Jews, who he blamed for most of Germany's problems. Despite this, he was backed by the majority of Germans, who were seduced by his charismatic speeches. Hitler's desire to increase German territory led to Germany's invasion of Czechoslovakia in 1938-1939, and then Poland in 1939. The latter invasion prompted Britain and France to declare war on Germany in September 1939. World War II had begun:

Adolf Hitler came to power in Germany with bold promises to revive the country's fortunes and increase its influence by expanding its territory.

1928, the country began to have ambitions of spreading the message of communism well beyond the borders of the USSR.

Germany and the rise of Hitler

After the defeat of Germany in World War I (1914–1918), the Allies imposed an extremely harsh punishment on the country. Germany was stripped of most of its wealth and ordered to pay compensation called reparations to the countries it had harmed during the conflict. This created enormous poverty in Germany, and great anger among its citizens who felt they were being punished too greatly for the mistakes of their leaders. To make matters worse, disastrous economic policies led to rampant inflation during the 1920s and early 1930s, when people found that a week's wages barely covered the cost of living. Responding to this desperation, the German dictator Adolf Hitler swept to power, promising to restore Germany to its former greatness. Hitler

PROPAGANDA *techniques*

Propaganda involves the spreading of ideas to promote or attack a cause. Stalin used propaganda as a tool to gain the backing of the people. He used the media to convince the Russian people and the people of East Germany of the dangers of capitalism, and to persuade them that the USSR was a strong, healthy nation capable of defeating this enemy. Posters, paintings and literature depicted the USSR as a place where the people were fit and happy, covering up the fact that millions of people who opposed Stalin were sent to their deaths during his reign.

> 'The death of a single individual is a tragedy. The death of a million is a statistic.'
>
> Stalin justifies the harsh policies of his government.

The Nazi-Soviet Pact

In 1939, an agreement called the Nazi-Soviet Pact was signed by the USSR and Germany. Under its terms, both countries promised to remain neutral if either country became involved in a conflict. However, two years later relations broke down and the two nations were at war with each other. In 1941, the Germans invaded the USSR and inflicted terrible damage on the country. Relations between the Soviets and the West also soured at this point because Stalin believed that the Allies had deliberately diverted the Nazis away from Western Europe and into the USSR. Hitler's troops were eventually driven back by Stalin's Red Army, and Germany found itself under attack from all directions. Forced to retreat to Berlin, Hitler found his army surrounded by troops from the USA, Britain and the USSR, and Germany was left with little choice but to surrender.

A clash of directions

When World War II ended, the victorious Allies had to decide what to do with the ruins of post-war Europe. In February 1945 they held a conference in Yalta. It re-established the nations destroyed by Hitler during the war, and carved Germany into four parts — one each for Britain, France, the USA and the USSR. In July, under the Potsdam Agreement, Germany was again made to pay for the atrocities that occurred under the Nazis. Each of the Allies could take money or goods from their part of Germany. But there was one issue still to be resolved — what to do with Berlin.

Berlin — the oasis

Situated in Soviet East Germany, Germany's capital presented Britain, France and the United States with a problem. They didn't want to give up their rights in Berlin but they were also wary of upsetting Stalin, as his Red Army massively outnumbered Allied forces in Berlin. Over a million Soviet troops had romped into the German capital in 1945, dwarfing the Allies' 50,000 soldiers.

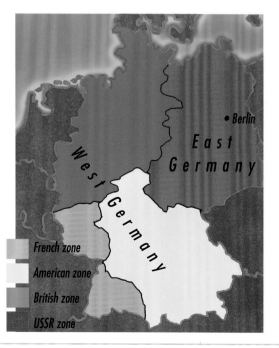

On October 6th, 1949, the Soviet sector became the German Democratic Republic, and the three Western powers merged their territories to create the Federal Republic of Germany. But while all sides agreed on this division, there was one issue still to be resolved — Berlin.

- French zone
- American zone
- British zone
- USSR zone

To solve the problem, Berlin was divided into four zones in the same way Germany itself had been split up. In 1948, Britain, France and the USA merged their areas together into a sector called West Berlin.

Stalin's plans

While the western powers were making plans in the other side of the city, Stalin began to rebuild the Soviet sector of Germany's capital as a socialist republic. The government controlled all economic activity and used the media in East Berlin and East Germany as a propaganda tool. Daily newspapers were heavily controlled by the state and dictated what the East Berliners should think and what views they should hold. This was in stark contrast to the free flow of information coming from the west of the city, where nearly 20 daily newspapers of all kinds of political views were in circulation.

Iron Curtain

The USSR had suffered more than anyone else during the war, losing 20 million soldiers and civilians. Because of this, there was great sympathy in the West for the Soviet Union. Stalin played on these feelings to gain Western approval for his idea that Eastern Europe would be recognized as part of the Soviet sphere of influence.

After the end of World War II, the USSR expanded its influence in Eastern Europe. The map above shows the 'Iron Curtain' – the countries under Soviet influence. Yugoslavia is grouped with the rest of the Iron Curtain countries because, despite the fact it was not under Soviet control and was not a member of the Warsaw pact, it was ruled by communists sympathetic to the USSR's world view.

After their victory, the Allies gathered at Yalta in the Ukraine to discuss the future of Europe. Agreements were made to restore countries such as Poland and Czechoslovakia, while Germany was to be divided up between Britain, France, the USA and the USSR.

NATO *and the Warsaw Pact*

As relations between East and West worsened, in 1949 the USA, Canada, and ten Western European nations arranged a guarantee of mutual defence and assistance in the North Atlantic Treaty Organization (NATO). In response, on May 1st, 1955, the USSR announced the birth of the Warsaw Pact, a treaty that bound the Eastern communist dictatorships into a single political and military force.

*This photograph (below) was taken at
the Potsdam conference. Seated (right
to left) are: Prime Minister Clement
Attlee of Great Britain; President Harry
S Truman; and Soviet Premier Joseph
Stalin. Standing in rear (left to right)
are: Admiral William Leahy, Chief of
Staff to President Truman; Hon. Ernest
Bevin, Britain's Foreign Minister; Sec. of
State James F Byrnes, US; and Russia's
Foreign Minister Vyacheslav Molotov.*

HUNGARY *crushed*

In 1956 Hungary's Prime Minister Nagy announced that he wanted the country to withdraw from the Warsaw Pact. However, the new Soviet leader Khrushchev was determined this would not happen so made an example of Hungary. He ordered 200,000 troops to be sent in to brutally crush the rebellion. Afterwards, Nagy was taken to Moscow and hanged as a traitor.

To combat any future threat from Germany, Stalin ensured that Poland, Hungary, Romania and Czechoslovakia – liberated by the Red Army from Nazism – converted to communism. This new area of influence became known as the 'Soviet Bloc' and the 'Iron Curtain', because it shut out Western Europe from the communist East.

The Truman Doctrine and the Marshall Plan

Although the United States was prepared to accept the USSR's influence in Eastern Europe, its leaders were determined that it should not extend its power any further. Two programs were set up to help contain communism. In 1947, the United States announced a plan called the Truman Doctrine. This was designed to help states going through a struggle for freedom against their oppressors. In the doctrine, President Truman committed America to assisting any country who felt their freedom being infringed by another country. The USA followed up the Truman Doctrine in 1948 with the Marshall Plan, an ambitious programme of economic aid. By pumping in massive amounts of money to help poor nations recover from the war, the idea was that the Marshall Plan would prevent any more countries coming under the control of the USSR. The plan had almost immediate success when American money helped prevent Italy from turning communist.

The impoverished East

After their division, the two sides of Berlin drifted further and further apart. West Germany and West Berlin turned their gaze completely to the Western world, joining the Council of Europe, the European Coal and Steel Community, NATO and the European Union. By contrast, Soviet East Germany and East Berlin became more isolated. Living standards slipped and people had to queue for basic provisions.

Berlin Blockade

As West Germany began to thrive, a growing number of East Germans began making their way to prosperous West Berlin to escape from the Soviet east. The situation became even worse when Britain, America and France introduced the deutschmark into West Berlin in 1948, making their side of the city an even more attractive place to live. This enraged Stalin, and on March 20th, 1948, Russia declared that it no longer recognized the Allied Control Council of Berlin. Stalin wanted the entire territory of Berlin under Soviet control. He decided to prevent Western forces reaching the capital by cutting off highways and railroads that led through through the Soviet-controlled territory into Berlin. The Berlin Blockade began in the middle of 1948, when Russian forces surrounded the city in an attempt to starve West Berlin into submission.

The Berlin Airlift
In response to the Blockade, the Allies began a dramatic and daring rescue plan called the Berlin Airlift. On June 21st, 1948, US and British planes began flying food and fuel into West Berlin, 24-hours-a-day, in order to keep the city alive. When the Soviets saw that the Allies did not intend to leave Berlin to surrender, they offered the citizens of West Berlin food and provisions in an attempt to bribe them into coming over to the east of the city. The move failed, however, and in May 1949, Russia was forced to admit defeat.

The GDR and the FRG
In 1949, Britain, France and the United States merged their zones of occupation to create a new country called the Federal Republic of Germany (West Germany). In response, the Soviet Union announced the formation of the German Democratic Republic (East Germany). The first Chancellor of the Federal Republic, Konrad Adenauer, refused to formally acknowledge the existence of East Germany, and relations between East and West deteriorated.

The brain drain
In 1949, the number of East Berliners escaping to West Berlin had reached 2,000 a week, but after the death of Stalin in 1953, it had soared to a staggering 6,000.

> 'I believe it must be the policy of the United States to support free peoples who are resisting attempted subjugation by armed minorities or by outside pressures.'
>
> **President Truman states his intentions in the Truman Plan.**

In total, an incredible 1.2 millions tons of supplies were dropped during the Berlin Blockade. The cargo required to keep Berlin going included coal, food, medical supplies, steamrollers, power-plant machinery, soap, and newsprint.

HEROES *of the airlift*

Airlift missions were extremely dangerous. Planes were landing and taking off every 90 seconds and pilots had just an hour and 40 minutes to get their planes refuelled, inspected and ready to go again. The pilot Bill Voigt's experiences were typical of many pilots. He flew to Berlin 116 times between July and November. 'You'd come in at a pretty steep angle. It's not a heck of a lot of space with a fully loaded airplane' said Voigt.

Another pilot, Ken Herman, remembered that 'when the weather was good you could see as many as six airplanes in front of you.' Accuracy was crucial, because if a pilot missed his approach, he had to turn around and take his cargo back to where he came from.

Incredibly, during the blockade, there were just 31 fatalities in a little under 200,000 flights.

THE FOUR *walls*

The 'Berlin Wall' was actually four walls built along the border between 1961 and 1989. The first was hastily erected on August 15th, 1961, and was made of a mixture of concrete and square blocks. In June 1962, a stronger wall was built to prevent people breaking through into the West. The third wall, begun in 1965, was far stronger and made of concrete slabs held between steel girders. The final wall was made of a new type of impenetrable concrete.

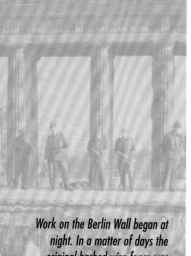

Work on the Berlin Wall began at night. In a matter of days the original barbed wire fence was torn down and replaced with a solid brick barrier (below).

Although the border between East and West Germany had been closed in 1952, East Germans could still escape the country by travelling to the refugee centre in Marienfelde, West Berlin. There, they had a choice: either to stay in West Berlin or catch a flight to another part of West Germany. East Berlin's leader, Walter Ulbricht, was alarmed that the country was losing the equivalent of a small town every year through West Berlin. He convinced the new leader of the USSR, Nikita Khrushchev, that it was time to take drastic action.

Tension at Vienna
In June 1961, Khrushchev met with the American President John F Kennedy in Vienna. The Soviet leader threatened that unless the Allies agreed to certain terms, he would force their troops out of the capital and seize total control of the city. Kennedy was furious and insisted that any action against West Berlin 'would result in war'. He flew to Berlin and, to show his support for the people of the city, declared 'Ich bin ein Berliner (I am a Berliner)'. Crucially however, he said nothing about the right of the Soviet Union to strengthen borders inside East Berlin.

The plan is hatched
After the failure to reach an agreement on the refugee situation in Vienna, a secret meeting was held between Ulbricht and the Kremlin. In a confidential memo from the future leader of East Germany, Erich Honecker, plans were made to erect a

physical barrier between East and West Berlin. By the evening of August 12th, 1961, rumours had begun to circulate about a plan to divide the city. Trains that were running into the East failed to come back again, and slowly Berlin's S-Bahn system ground to a halt. Taxi drivers in West Berlin started refusing to take people to the east of the city, and people who visited the Brandenburg Gate that night were refused access.

Building the Wall
Early on the morning of August 15th, 1961, the GDR began to block off the east of the city from the west. At first the barrier was marked only by barbed wire, but soon afterwards, the people of East Berlin were forced at gunpoint to help troops put up a 154-kilometre concrete barrier. Most of the work was done at night to create the minimum of fuss. People living in houses along the line were issued with compulsory evacuation orders. If they were not out by the time specified, they were told that their houses would be bricked up with them still inside. On August 23rd, 1961, citizens of West Berlin were told that they would no longer be allowed to enter East Berlin. The Soviets responded to any criticism by referring to the new barrier as an 'anti-fascist protection wall'.

Dividing a city Berlin's division wove its way through at least 60 major roads — over graveyards, across railway stations, and even through the middle of one house. Factories,

apartment blocks and anything else that got in the way of the Wall's path were hauled down. Even Berlin's famous S-Bahn train system was broken up. Over 300 watchtowers were built to guard a strip of land set up as a barrier between the Wall and the rest of East Germany.

Checkpoint Charlie
Nine days after the Wall went up, East Germany tried to stop Britain, the USA and France from gaining access to East Berlin. They closed five checkpoints between the two halves of the city, one of which was the sector-crossing point at Friedrichstrasse. On September 22nd, 1961, the USA set up a temporary checkpoint near Friedrichstrasse. It was named Checkpoint Charlie after the two checkpoints on the freeway leading to Berlin — Alpha (Helmstedt) and Bravo (Dreilinden). Until 1990, Checkpoint Charlie was the only crossing point for foreigners between East and West Berlin.

Checkpoint Charlie was a potential flashpoint where East came directly into contact with West. A white line painted across the road signified exactly where the influence of the United States and their Allies ended.

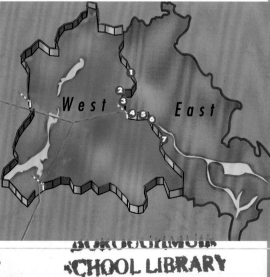

The Berlin Wall stretched for almost 160 kilometres around the city. An amazing 106 kilometres of the concrete barrier towered four metres high. The Berlin Wall was protected by over 300 watchtowers and 20 bunkers.
1. Bornholmer Strasse
2. Chausseestrasse
3. Invaliden Strasse
4. Checkpoint Charlie
5. Heinrich-Heine-Strasse
6. Oberbaumbrücke
7. Sonnenallee

It took the people of Berlin many years to adjust to the Wall, and some never came to terms with the divide. Sadly, the Wall is famous for the numbers who lost their lives trying to scramble over, dig under and find other ways to breach it. By the end of the 1960s, however, the political landscape of the world was changing, and the future of the Berlin Wall was looking less certain.

East German guards carry away the lifeless body of Peter Fechter.

August 1961

In August 1961, as the barbed-wire barriers were being replaced with a brick wall, people burrowed under houses on the border to make their escapes, wriggling through tunnels to the sanctuary of the West. The East German Rudolf Urban was attempting to cross the divide through a house in Bernauer Strasse when workmen began bricking up the doors and windows. Urban's friend got out in time, but Urban fell from a window and broke his ankle. He was taken to an East German hospital for examination but, mysteriously, he was later reported dead. By the end of August, the East German authorities had hardened their attitudes towards attempted escapes, and a 'shoot-to-kill policy' was in operation at the border. On 4 October 1961, a student called Bernard Lanser jumped from the roof of a house in Bernauer Strasse, but landed awkwardly. He was gunned down by border guards, while a man who had tried to help him flee was beaten to death. Eventually, the authorities ordered residents in streets like Bernauer Strasse to find somewhere else to live, because the closeness of their houses to the wall made them a popular escape route. People were forced to come up with ever more cunning ways to beat the border guards. One 33-year-old East German hired an American soldier's outfit from a fancy dress shop in East Berlin,

PETER *Fechter*

The most famous casualty of the Berlin Wall was 18-year-old Peter Fechter. He had hatched a plan with a friend to climb over the wall from a building in Zimmerstrasse. Fechter's friend made it over but Fechter was shot, and collapsed back onto the eastern side, just 50 metres (167 feet) from freedom. He was left bleeding to death for nearly an hour before the authorities took him away.

and managed to walk through Checkpoint Charlie unnoticed. Another used a high-powered sportscar with the windscreen removed to race under the barriers. Other escapees resorted to cruder methods. A group of East Germans used a truck reinforced with steel and concrete to ram through a checkpoint in front of bewildered guards.

October 1962 The Cold War exploded into life in October 1962 when an American spy

VIETNAM

The Vietnam War was a battle between the US-backed Republic of Vietnam in the south, and the Communist Democratic Republic of Vietnam in the north. The war lasted from the mid-1950s until 1973 when, against all the odds, American troops withdrew. South Vietnam then surrendered in 1975. The Vietnam War was important in relation to the Cold War because it made the United States realise that it could not stop the spread of communism. Discussion and negotiation with the East was the best course of action, rather than military aggression.

plane flying over Cuba photographed several suspected military sites. The photographs proved that the Soviets were building military bases in Cuba that were capable of firing nuclear missiles at the USA. Cuba's communist president Fidel Castro was a friend of the Soviet Union, and President Kennedy was fearful of what might happen. Kennedy had organized a failed coup in 1961 against the Cuban leader, and he knew that Castro hated the USA . Kennedy placed a naval blockade around Cuba and forced Kruschchev to withdraw his missiles. In return, the USA promised not to invade Cuba. Kennedy and Kruschchev also set up a special telephone connection between the two countries to prevent a war from beginning by mistake. Relations thawed again in August 1963 when the countries signed an agreement not to test any more nuclear bombs.

January 1968
In January 1968, Alexander Dubcek was elected as the new leader of Czechoslovakia. During what became known as the Prague Spring, Dubcek announced a series of reforms that included the abolition of censorship and the right of Czech citizens to criticize their government.

When Fidel Castro and his comrades swept to power in Cuba on January 1st, 1959, he was the youngest leader on the planet, aged just 32. Castro is so revered in Cuba that his full name is hardly ever spoken there in public — most people call him Fidel or just touch their chin to indicate his beard.

Over the next four months, Dubcek worked hard to convince the Soviet Union that Czechoslovakia would remain within the Soviet Bloc and that there would not be a return to capitalism. Despite these assurances, however, the USSR was alarmed and on August 20th, Soviet troops invaded the country. In contrast to the Soviet invasion of Hungary 12 years earlier, the invasion of Czechoslovakia did not meet armed resistance, but Russian troops faced jeering crowds who showed no warmth towards their communist masters.

1971 Ostpolitik was a policy developed by Willy Brandt, chancellor of West Germany, to try to improve relations between the East and West. In 1971, the policy led to an agreement called the Basic Treaty. In it the Federal Republic of Germany and German Democratic Republic committed themselves to developing normal relations and recognizing each other's borders. Under Ostpolitik, the Federal Republic of Germany also exchanged ambassadors with the Soviet Union, Poland, Czechoslovakia, Hungary and Bulgaria.

1972 Relations between the USA and the USSR improved dramatically in 1972. A meeting called the SALT (Strategic Arms Limitation Talks) conference was held to discuss limiting the number of nuclear missiles produced by both superpowers. It was followed up by the Helsinki Accord which contained important human rights legislation. A further SALT meeting was planned for 1979. However, on Christmas Day, 1979 the USSR invaded Afghanistan and, in protest, the United States suspended talks and even refused to attend the 1980 Olympic Games in Moscow.

1978 In 1978, the East German government acknowledged that it needed help from the West to fight off poverty, despite its earlier insistence that it would remain totally detached from the West. Erich Honecker, the East German leader, agreed to the implementation of human rights reforms in return for economic aid. In 1984, East Germany dismantled guns along its border with West Germany in return for two large loans.

By the 1970s, America and the USSR had stockpiled hundreds of nuclear weapons between them. Just a handful would have been enough to wipe the entire human race off the face of the planet.

BANKRUPTING *the USSR*

In 1983, President Reagan announced plans for a nuclear-defence programme called SDI that would blow up enemy missiles in space before they reached their target. The plan was never implemented, but it made the USSR realize that it could never keep up with America's defence plans. Then in 1988, Soviet forces were driven out of Afghanistan by a rebel force called the mujahedin, aided by the USA. The USSR's status as a superpower was disintegrating.

WALL ART *on the western side*

During the 1980s, many artists started to paint on the western side of the Wall. In stark contrast, however, the eastern side of the Wall remained untouched as graffiti artists knew they risked being shot if they entered the strip of no-man's-land to reach the Wall. However, after its collapse in 1989, artists finally began to make their mark on the eastern side of the Wall. Today, only a few painted sections of the former Berlin Wall remain, but a gallery has been set up with a permanent display of Wall art.

> '*Mr Gorbachev tear down this wall!*'
>
> **US President Ronald Reagan challenges Gorbachev to end the division of Berlin in 1987**

1981

In 1981, the former movie actor Ronald Reagan was elected as the new American president. Naturally suspicious of the USSR, he vowed to get tough with the Soviets and with what he referred to as 'the evil empire'. However, Reagan was surrounded by advisors who urged him to adopt a more peaceful relationship with the USSR. This appealed to the president because he saw arms reduction as a way of saving money, allowing him to make the tax cuts he had promised to the American people when he ran for president.

1982

Helmut Kohl became Chancellor of the Federal Republic of Germany in October, 1982. A large, confident man, he refused to keep apologizing for Germany's actions in the past. Instead he encouraged the people of his country to look to the future. Kohl was the driving force behind later plans for German reunification and, along with President Mitterrand of France, for greater unity in Europe.

1985

In 1985, Mikhail Gorbachev was elected as the new leader of the USSR. Gorbachev introduced new ideas into Russian politics such as Glasnost (greater freedom of speech) and Perestroika (reform of the economy to allow profit-making). Gorbachev's firm belief was that change 'was knocking at every door and window', and that 'life punishes those who come too late'. His willingness to talk and deal with situations calmly where previous leaders would have responded with bullets and tanks helped end the Cold War. Gorbachev allowed a clutch of countries to leave the Soviet Bloc peacefully (*see page 20–21*), and respected the right of individuals to choose their own destiny. On October 7th, 1989, Gorbachev urged Erich Honecker to carry out reforms in East Germany, appealing for 'brave decisions' from the leader.

In 1984, Mikhail Gorbachev was elected as the new leader of the USSR. He was a relatively young man born after the Russian Revolution, and his glamourous wife Raisa loved to dress in Western clothes.

Austria became a haven for East Germans after its borders with Hungary were thrown open.

May 1989 In May 1989, communist Hungary made the momentous decision to dismantle its wire border with Austria. For years a favourite destination for East German holidaymakers, the opening up of Hungary helped tens of thousands to make their escape to the West. Anyone wanting to leave the communist East could now simply travel to the Hungarian border, disappear into the woodlands and scurry across the border to Austria. Once there, they could carry on to West Germany where they would automatically became West German citizens. By the end of September, an incredible 30,000 East Berliners had made their escape through Hungary.

August 1989 Other people started heading for the Federal Republic's consulate in East Berlin. On August 8th, the building had to be closed because the number of refugees turning up at its doors was spiralling out of control. When this happened, people started heading instead for the FRG's consulate in Budapest, Hungary and as a result, this also closed. Later, refugees swamped the FRG Embassy in Prague, Czechoslovakia, and were authorized to emigrate by the Czech government.

June 1988 The East German leader Honecker was, for many years, unrepentant about the hundreds of people killed trying to escape to the West. He expressed regret only for his '25 comrades who have been treacherously murdered at the border'. Honecker suspended the shoot-to-kill policy at the Wall during special state occasions, but tragically, the deaths continued. Chris Gueffroy, a 20-year-old waiter, was the last to be shot by border guards on February 5th, 1989. His death provoked a storm of international outrage, but it also marked a moment of real change. Gueffroy's family were allowed to place a funeral notice in East German newspapers, something that had never happened before, and the funeral was attended by Western media who published photographs of the event across the world.

June 1989 The mood for change in East Germany was also reflected by developments elsewhere in communist Europe. In 1988, the ruling Communist Party in Poland faced a wave of strikes that brought the country to its knees. In June 1989, the Polish head-of-state, General Jaruzelski, was forced to lift the ban on the workers union Solidarity and call free elections. In Poland's first poll for over 30 years, Solidarity stormed to victory, with Tadeusz Mazowiecki elected as Eastern Europe's first non-communist leader.

LEIPZIG *church*

Local elections held in East Germany on May 7th, 1989 provoked more unrest with allegations of vote-rigging began. Protesters made their way to the Nikolai Church in Leipzig where a crowd of 20,000 marched to Karl Marx Square. Amazingly, the military took no action against the protestors.

October 1989 Gorbachev was due to visit East Berlin in October for the 40th anniversary celebrations of the GDR's founding. This frightened East Berlin's rulers. Fearing a mass demonstration on the Western side of the city against Gorbachev's presence, the border guards began to put up a new, reinforced wall at Checkpoint Charlie to keep protesters from the West out and its own people in. When Gorbachev arrived in the German capital on a hot October day in 1989, he was greeted with demonstrators on the streets of East Berlin, pleading 'Gorby, help us! Gorby, help us'. In the Western side of the city, border guards were pelted with bottles and eggs by angry crowds. When Gorbachev left Berlin, the new wall at Checkpoint Charlie was torn down, but the political mood had changed forever. Protestors had been allowed to demonstrate without the threat of violent repression. Erich Honecker, a hardened opponent of Gorbachev's reforms, had declared that 'the Wall will still be standing in 50 or 100 years if the reasons for its existence are not removed'. But his beliefs were becoming increasingly outdated. On October 18th, 1989, he was deposed by reformers in his own party, and

The East German leader Erich Honecker and his wife Margot. His opposition to any talk about pulling down the Berlin Wall was making him increasingly unpopular.

replaced by Egon Krenz who inherited a country which was virtually bankrupt. Instead of using the weapon of fear to force citizens to stay in Berlin, he pleaded with his people: 'Your place is here. We need you'. To appease the increasing number of demonstrators, the Politburo announced that from November 1st, 1989, East Germans would be allowed to travel to the West for a maximum of 30 days.

During a visit from Pope John Paul II, Polish demonstrators gathered to protest at the banning of the Solidarity trade union. The trade union had became a national movement backed even by the Roman Catholic Church in Poland, though it was made illegal by the Polish government from 1981 to 1989.

THE NEW FORUM *movement*

After Hungary opened its borders, a handful of East German activists formed a group called the New Forum, which was a place to air views on reform in East Germany. Weekly meetings and radio broadcasts took place and a manifesto for reform was put together.

00:00

A CRITICAL SITUATION

At midnight on November 9th, 1989, an incredible 1,000 East Germans fled to West Germany via Czechoslovakia. A vast tide of people made their way to Western embassies in Prague, from where they could re-register as West German citizens. Alarmed at the scale of the exodus, the Krenz government called a press conference to announce a new travel law which they hoped would tackle the problem.

Gunter Schabowski, the man chosen to make the momentous announcement.

Schabowski was visibly nervous after the news conference.

By November 1989, the divisions between East and West Germany were already fragmenting, and on the night of 9 November, the wall started to crumble. Following a speech by a government official called Gunter Schabowski, border restrictions were effectively lifted, and people began to make their way in their thousands towards the checkpoints.

THE CHOSEN MAN

17:40

Around 5.40 pm, the Berlin Party Secretary, Gunter Schabowski, met with Prime Minister Krenz to discuss the press conference scheduled for 6.00 pm. Krenz passed Schabowski a document with the new travel law written on it, telling him, 'Announce this. It will be a bombshell'. Flustered by recent events, however, Schabowski failed to read the script properly.

THE CONFERENCE BEGINS

18:57

At the end of the news conference, Schabowski announced that East Germany was lifting all travel restrictions. 'Private trips abroad can be applied for without questions, and ... the People's Police have been instructed to hand out long-term exit visas without delay.' A journalist asked Schabowski when the new regulation would take effect. He stammered, 'As far as I know, this enters into force ... this is immediately, without delay.' Schabowski was questioned again by a journalist and he repeated that 'permanent emigration can take place at all GDR border crossing points to the Federal Republic and West Berlin.' It is unlikely that Schabowski had any idea of what he had just said. When he was asked by a journalist later if the law would lead to mass emigration, he replied, 'I hope it doesn't come to that.'

NEWSFLASHES

19:01

Just four minutes after Schabowski had finished his speech, the world's major news agencies had already seized on his comments, and were sending frantic newsflashes around the globe. While Reuters announced the fact that there would be new travel arrangements, the Associated Press agency went much further, speculating that the borders would be coming down immediately.

VIEWS *from the ground*

'We had no warning of what he was going to say, although we thought something might happen. We made up our minds we had understood it correctly, and that he had opened the wall: we replayed a video of it just to make sure. And then, of course, everybody was very busy writing, and writing, and writing.'

Journalist Erdmute Greis-Behrendt reacting to Schabowski's speech.

'A young man... was waving at us. "Hey folks, you know what? The borders are open! Isn't this weird?!" How can this work, I ask myself. Will we be the last ones to turn out the light in the GDR then? Will everyone go west now that it shall be so easy? This sounds so incredible that I can hardly grasp it.'

East German Thomas Khalou's reaction to the reporting of Schabowski's speech.

BORNHOLMER STRASSE CHECKPOINT

19:05

While the world's media had already decided about the fate of Berlin's Wall, passport officials in East Berlin remained sceptical. Harald Jaeger, the man in charge of passport control at the Bornholmer Strasse checkpoint, refused to accept that Schabowski had made anything other than a mistake. 'What does this Schabowski mean by "immediately"? That is simply not possible.'

VIEWS *from the ground*

'Looking around I saw an indescribable joy in people's faces. It was the end of the government telling people what not to do, it was the end of the Wall, the end of the war and of East and West.'

An East German writes about his joy at the events.

'Everything was out of control. Police on horses watched powerless. To get a better view, people were climbing onto shops on the West Side.'

Rainer Pterck, a visitor to Berlin, describes the scenes.

THE NEWS ON THE NEWS `19:30`

The German television channel ZDF broadcast the news of Schabowski's speech at 7.17 pm, but it was only the sixth item on their bulletin. At 7.30 pm, the GDR programme *Aktuelle Kamera* reported the event as their second item, and word started to spread. Then the eight o'clock broadcast on West Germany's ARD evening news reported that the border was completely open.

BORNHOLMER STRASSE `20:00`

By the time Schabowski's speech had begun broadcasting on national television, the number of people gathering at Bornholmer Strasse had grown from a steady trickle to a deluge. By 8.30 pm there were thousands of people at the checkpoint, because, unlike Checkpoint Charlie, Bornholmer Strasse was situated in a busy residential area.

Just an hour after the announcement, queues started to build at Bornholmer Strasse checkpoint.

PRESSURE BUILDS

By 9.00 pm the crowd had grown to tens of thousands. A queue of cars snaked several hundred metres down the main road, spilling over into the side streets as well. The head of passport control, Harald Jaeger, telephoned headquarters, and was told to let any troublemakers through to defuse the situation. The plan was to stamp their identity cards in such a way that they would not be able to return to East Berlin. By 9.20 pm several hundred had been allowed through the three passport huts at the border into West Berlin, while the crowds left behind chanted 'Open the gates, open the gates'.

Crowds jostle for the best viewpoint at Bornholmer Strasse.

CHECKPOINT CHARLIE

At the same time as people were massing at Bornholmer Strasse, a crowd of a few hundred had gathered on the western side of Checkpoint Charlie. They urged the guards to let the people on the other side come through into West Berlin, but were politely refused. By 10.00 pm, a few people stepped out of the crowd and stepped over the dividing line, technically crossing onto East German territory. They were gently pushed back by border guards, who were still being told by the authorities that there were no changes to the status of the wall.

VOUS S... DU SECTEUR AMÉRICAIN

SIE VERLASSEN DEN AMERIKANISCHEN SEKTOR
US ARMY

People in West Berlin begin to test the resolve of border guards at Checkpoint Charlie.

VIEWS *from the ground*

'I am just so happy. Berlin is Berlin again! Now finally this hated wall has been smashed down and we can be together again. I have friends and family in the East that I haven't seen for years,'

Jurgen Schwarker from West Berlin.

'I just can't believe it! I don't feel like I'm in prison anymore!'

Angelika Wache, 34, the first visitor to cross at Checkpoint Charlie.

'Go have a beer.'

A West Berliner to Torsten Ryl, one of many who came over just to see what the West was like, as he handed Ryl a 20-mark bill.

WE CAN'T HOLD FOR MUCH LONGER   `22:45`

In ARD's nightly news broadcast, an announcement was made that 'the gates in the Wall are open' despite the fact that the checkpoints were still physically shut. Pressure was becoming unbearable at the border crossings and it was growing more and more difficult for guards to keep increasingly restless crowds in order.

UP ON THE WALL   `22:50`

At Checkpoint Charlie, the attitudes of the men chosen to guard the crossing point were visibly changing. Bewildered by what was happening, they decided to disobey an order to close the pedestrian gate at Checkpoint Charlie. People began to stream over towards the Wall, and started climbing on to it. Major Bernie Godek of the US Army recorded that 'people were sitting on the wall with their legs draped down, almost lolled, casual as you like.' As this was happening, many of the guards were removing their helmets and joining in with the sea of people pressing up against the Wall, even agreeing to take photographs for West Germans.

Guards at many of the checkpoints were buckling under the pressure (above).

People began climbing onto the Wall at various checkpoints.

Bornholmer Strasse was one of the first checkpoints to open.

CHECKPOINT CHARLIE   `00:00`

At Checkpoint Charlie, East German commander Gunter Moll was faced with a baying crowd from both directions. In East Berlin, the crowd were shouting 'Let us go! Let us go!', while in West Berlin, the thousands were urging 'Come! Come! Come!'. At one minute to midnight, Moll made the decision to open the pedestrian gate.

ONE OF THE FIRST   `23:00`

In East Berlin, the pressure continued to build. A crowd of almost 20,000 people were pressing up against Bornholmer Strasse checkpoint, encouraged by news that the Rudower Chaussee checkpoint in the south of the city had been opened. A noisy chant of 'Open it! Open it!' began. As Harald Jaeger realised the danger of holding back such a huge number of people, he made the order to 'Open them all'. These three words unleashed a jubilant torrent of people from East to West. At 11.35 pm, the Heinrich-Heine-Strasse checkpoint further south was also opened.

People began pouring through Checkpoint Charlie at midnight.

`10:11:89`

As the new day arrived, people began celebrating with bewildered border guards.

CHECKPOINT CHARLIE `00:50`

By midnight, all the border guards had abandoned their posts and begun to mingle with the crowd. Realizing that they had lost control and that what they thought they had been protecting just didn't matter any more, they threw away their guns. Overcome by the joyous atmosphere, they celebrated the freedom of the city with the other revellers. Drinks were passed freely amongst the crowds, and for the first time in 28 years, no-one cared what side of Berlin they came from. They were all Berliners, and nothing else mattered.

`01:35`

BORNHOLMER STRASSE

The thousands who had massed at Bornholmer Strasse let out a roar and started going through the checkpoint, as well as up and over the Wall. West Berliners pulled East Berliners to the top of the barrier where, in years past, people trying to cross over had been shot. At 1.35 am, Chris Toft of the British Military Police reported that people 'were chipping away at the Wall with hammers'. These would soon be replaced with bulldozers.

Angry Berliners began chipping away at the wall.

VIEWS *from the ground*

'Over 20,000 East and West Germans were gathered in a huge party … Between lanes of cars, a group of musicians were playing violins and accordions, and men and women were dancing in circles.'

East German Gunter Hanski remembers the night the Wall fell.

'In front of the Brandenburg Gate, the wall measured four feet across, so there was enough room for hundreds of people to stand and drink. Women beseeched guards: 'Come up here! Drink! Dance! It's all over! Forget the damned wall! Forget the GDR!' I never tired of watching Germans fall into each other's arms.'

Henry Porter in "The Brandenburg Gate Opens".

ANGER IN THE EAST

In the capital of East Germany, huge crowds began to celebrate the collapse of the Wall, hoping that it would bring East and West Germany together again. They were also angry at the lies they had been told for years by their government, and began to demonstrate. Revellers set fire to cars draped in the East German flag and chanted for the reunification of Germany. Eventually, the crowds started to disperse as more and more people headed west to see what was going on in the heart of Berlin. Many East Germans were desperate to meet up with friends and family on the other side, some of who they had not seen for years.

Many vehicles were destroyed in East Germany as people expressed their anger at their government.

BRANDENBURG GATE

Two hours later, visitors from the West had started coming into the other side of Berlin. Many headed for the Brandenburg Gate, a point right on the dividing line. People were climbing up and dancing on its wall while guards looked on.

FREE MOVEMENT

As dawn broke in Berlin, cars were moving freely from East to West. Many East Germans were returning home after a giddy night in the West. After years of having to exist on the most basic food, Eastern shoppers loaded up their bags with fruit, cigarettes and electrical goods. Many were simply unable to believe what they found in the West, where supermarket shelves groaned with every imaginable luxury. 'Going to West Berlin was as good as going to Australia for me', said one East German.

East Germans returned laden with shopping.

'**D**evelopments are now unforeseeable,' said West German Chancellor Helmut Kohl. 'The wheel of history is turning faster now.' By early 1990, the prospect of reunification was become more and more likely. Kohl was becoming increasingly vocal in his demands to unite the states, while in the East, Prime Minister Modrow was forced by public unrest to start thinking about the prospect of a single Germany.*

In December 1989, West and East West German Chancellor Helmut Kohl and East German President Hans Modrow met at Dresden, in East Germany to discuss greater co-operation between the two countries. Barely a year later, the two halves of Germany would be reunited again.

Last remnants

By the evening of November 11th, the first concrete slabs were being removed. On the following day, the borders were finally flung open at Potsdamer Platz – once one of the busiest crossroads in Europe. The West Berlin Philharmonic Orchestra played to mark the event.

Kohl and Gorbachev

While the Berlin Wall was being torn down, Chancellor Helmut Kohl was visiting the Polish Prime Minister in Warsaw. When news reached him about events during the night, he left early the next morning and flew to Berlin to attend a rally there. As Kohl waited to speak, he received a telephone call from the Soviet Ambassador in Berlin, who had a message from Mikhail Gorbachev. The Russian leader wanted to know if citizens were attacking Soviet bases in East Germany. Realising that Gorbachev was being fed false information by his political opponents in Russia who were opposed to any reform, Kohl told an aide to reassure the Soviet leader that there was no truth to any of these rumours.

Tourists to the West

After the collapse of the Wall, an estimated two million East Germans visited West Germany. Day passes were issued to anyone wanting to travel to West Berlin, and thousands of people piled on to free trains laid on by the West German government. One visitor observed that 'more than 80% of East Germany was

TRABI *cars*

When the Wall fell in 1989, West Berliners saw hundreds of odd looking cars puttering out from the east of the city. These plastic and fibreglass vehicles were called Trabants, or 'Trabi' cars. With a top speed of 99 km/h (62 mph), and a tiny but noisy engine that sounded more like a motorbike, the Trabi seemed hopelessly primitive when compared to Western cars. Today, they are remembered with affection, and an international meeting for ex-Trabi owners attracts thousands of visitors every year.

in vacation in West Germany'. Universities in East Germany were forced to cancel lessons as it soon became apparent that all their students were deserting classes in order to visit the West. Once there, East Berliners could visit any bank to get 100 deutschmarks of 'Welcome Money', the equivalent of several months wages in the East. They also found volunteers in the streets handing out cakes to the Easterners, thinking them so poor that they couldn't afford to eat.

Collapse of the Soviet Bloc

The fall of the Berlin Wall set off a ripple that reverberated around Europe. In December 1989, the former Solidarity leader Lech Walesa was elected president of Poland. In the same month, the Communist Party in Czechoslovakia resigned as a result of a mass demonstration on November 17th, 1989. In Hungary, the ruling Communist Party dissolved and announced free elections to take place in March 1990. In Romania, a bloody revolution took place in December in which the communist dictator Nicolae Ceausescu and his wife Elena were executed. In less than six months, the Iron Curtain had vanished.

Hans Modrow

In East Germany, the newly elected Prime Minister Hans Modrow caught the mood by proposing 'a community of treaties' to increase co-operation between the two Germanies. However, he still believed that East and West Germany should stay as two nations, despite the fact that East Germans continued to desert their country and head westwards.

SELLING *the Wall*

Just a few weeks after the Wall had fallen, it was being sold in pieces to eager tourists. Stalls operated by East Germans, Poles and Turks quickly sprung up along the path of the fallen barrier. Tourists wanted painted pieces of the sections from the eastern side, so the sellers sprayed them up to get a better price. It was also possible to buy genuine East German and Soviet army uniforms. Today, it is still possible to buy fragments of the Wall both in Germany and all over the world via the Internet.

The population in Prague celebrated wildly after hearing that the Czech Communist Party resigned on November 24th, 1989.

> *'I am sure unity will come if the German people want it.'*
>
> German Chancellor
> Helmut Kohl

THE STASI's *reign of terror*

'Stasi' was the name for the notorious East German secret police. They arrested political opponents and threw anyone who disagreed with political policies into prison. The full extent of the Stasi's chilling reign of terror only become evident when the Berlin Wall fell in 1989. As the communist regime collapsed, Stasi officials frantically tried to destroy incriminating documents but were caught before they could do so.

Victims of the Stasi gather in Leipzig, East Germany, on December 18th, 1989. Regular demonstrations were held outside the Stasi building because people feared the hated secret police were about to launch a new crackdown in East Germany.

Coming down to earth

In West Germany, people's attitude towards the Ossies (Easterners) began to change as the jubilation was replaced by day-to-day reality. Millions of East Germans flooded into West Berlin every weekend and locals found their streets blocked as Trabant cars coughed their way down city streets. They also faced long queues at banks behind Easterners waiting to collect their welcome money. Many West Berliners were losing patience with their neighbours and many East Germans also felt that they had lost their dignity when the Wall went down. One remarked, 'I feel like a beggar if I go to take my 100 marks'.

Aid for elections

On November 28th, 1989, Helmut Kohl announced for the first time that he wanted to unite the two Germanys. He made an offer to East Germany that West Germany would provide millions of pounds of economic aid in return for free elections in East Berlin.

Resistance abroad

Kohl's plans for reunification received a mixed reaction abroad. In Britain, Prime Minister Margaret Thatcher was alarmed about the prospect of a united Germany, and wished to 'check the German juggernaut'. In France, President Mitterrand was furious at Kohl's plans but confident that the USSR would never allow such a thing to happen.
'I don't have to oppose it –

THE *STASI files*

Stasi files revealed that the secret police had 85,000 full-time employees plus half a million informants who were employed to find out everything that was going on in East Germany. Over one-third of all East Germans were spied on by the Stasi, and investigators found a massive collection of reports that are still being sifted through. After the fall of the Wall, all Germans were allowed access to their files. Many were astonished to find that family members and close friends had in fact been spying on them. The files also revealed the hypocrisy of East German society. While the ordinary people of communist East Germany lived austere lives, leaders such as Erich Honecker owned lavish hunting lodges complete with staff, and took expensive holidays in the West.

The commissioner's archives house in Berlin has an incredible 122 kilometres of Stasi files. More than 1.7 million Germans have visited the building to inspect their files, and many have been shocked at what they found.

the Soviets will do it for me', he declared. Only the USA supported the idea of unification from the start. Although he didn't want to inflame the USSR by 'dancing on the Wall', President George Bush (Sr) said that he had no fear of the prospect of a united Germany.

Chaos in the East

By the end of 1989, the political situation in East Germany was becoming increasingly unstable. Mass emigration was continuing and the national currency was sinking fast. Although a few intellectuals campaigned for an independent East Germany, most East Germans were increasingly in favour of unification.

End of the Stasi

On November 20th, 1989 thousands of East Germans marched through Leipzig, chanting, 'We are the people'. They feared that the ruling party was trying to increase its power – a suspicion that grew when the communists held a large 'anti-fascist rally' in January. When Prime Minister Modrow announced plans to replace the hated Stasi with a new secret police force, furious East Germans decided to take action. On January 15th, 1990, furious protesters stormed the Stasi headquarters in East Berlin, and tore the building apart, daubing the walls with anti-communist slogans.

Kohl meets Gorbachev

Chancellor Kohl was aware that if reunification was to become a reality, he needed to convince the USSR of his plans. On February 10th, 1990, he set off for Moscow for a meeting with Gorbachev. After Kohl had reassured Gorbachev that current borders would not be infringed, or that Soviet trade with East Germany would not be affected, the Russian leader told the German that there were 'no differences of opinion ... about unity and the people's right to seek it'. Kohl flew home triumphant and in a television broadcast, he announced that the USSR would not oppose German unification.

PHYSICAL *symbols removed*

In Berlin itself, just a few months after the fall of the Wall, the physical symbols of division were being removed at a startling rate. Lenin's statue was removed from Leninplatz, East Berlin, and a huge crane lifted up and destroyed the Allied hut at Checkpoint Charlie to the sounds of a marching band.

Modrow's free elections

On February 1st, 1990, the prime minister of East Germany, Hans Modrow, decided to do a U-turn and back reunification, declaring 'the unification of the two German states is now on the agenda'. Then, on March 18th, East Germany held its first free elections. Most of the parties standing were backed by political groups from the West, including the 'Alliance for Germany' party, backed by Kohl himself. The favourites, the SPD, made several

On the day Germany was finally reunited, hundreds of thousands of East and West Germans massed in the centre of Berlin.

mistakes along the way, including an announcement by a former member that he was 'an alternative Marxist'. Desperate not to re-elect a communist-style government, voters got behind Kohl's party, tempted by his slogan: 'Without Kohl, no cash'.

Reunification

Now that parties on both sides of Germany backed reunification, the final step was to come up with an agreement that would replace an unsigned peace treaty drawn up by the Allies at the end of World War II. On July 16th, 1990, Kohl signed an agreement with the Allies called the Two (Germanies) Plus Four (Allies) Treaty. It ended the Allies' rights in Germany, and allowed the

MORE *celebrations*

Many East and West Germans were completely overwhelmed when it was announced that Germany would again be one nation. One East German woman, Ursula Grosser Dixon, said, 'I completely lost my composure. People were singing the German national anthem in the streets. As tired as I was, I have never enjoyed a celebration more in my life.'

new Germany to remain in NATO, as long as its authority didn't extend to former East Germany while Soviet troops were still stationed there. These troops would be withdrawn after four years. There was also a commitment by Germany not to obtain a nuclear arsenal. Then at midnight on October 3rd, 1990, Germany was officially reunited, less than 11 months after the Wall had come crashing down.

Berlin or Bonn?

Now the new German government had to decide where the new capital should be. The two options that were considered were Bonn, the capital of the old West Germany and Berlin, East Germany's capital and Germany's historic first city. Bonn was so far away from old East Germany that the government decided its selection would have made the citizens of the eastern state feel excluded from the political process. So, in 1991, Berlin was selected and made the new capital city. Gradually, the government offices and activities were moved from Bonn to Berlin. The move was finally completed in 2000.

War crimes trials

Attention now focused on those who had committed terrible crimes against people trying to cross the Wall. In September 1991, four former border guards were convicted of killing Chris Gueffroy, despite their pleas that they were only obeying orders. The former prime minister Erich Honecker was also arrested in Moscow and sent back to Germany. Charged with manslaughter because of his 'shoot-to-kill' policy, Honecker only escaped jail because he was terminally ill. Egon Krenz received a six-and-a-half year sentence in 1997, while Schabowski was sentenced to three years in prison.

Egon Krenz, the former prime minister of the GDR, received a six-and-a-half year sentence for his part in the crimes committed during the communist regime.

'The Soviet Union will respect the decision of the Germans to live in one state, and that it is up to the Germans to decide themselves the time and the way to unite.'

Chancellor Kohl

After reunification, rapid change continued in Germany and in the rest of Europe. Just two years after the fall of the Berlin Wall, the USSR collapsed, while at home, a wave of immigrants attracted to the new Germany led to the emergence of Neo-Nazi groups in the old FRG. Wars in Europe and the Middle East also tested Germany's new foreign policy, while the nation also played a crucial role in the shaping of a new Europe.

Part of the Reichstag building features a glass and steel dome from which visitors can look down into the parliamentary chamber. The building's design is meant to reflect Germany's commitment to more visible government.

Collapse of the USSR

Because Gorbachev had allowed countries in the Soviet Bloc to leave peacefully, many hardliners at home were furious. They began plotting to remove him and in 1991, seized power in a coup, imprisoning the Russian leader. However, street protests, led by the future president Boris Yeltsin, ended the coup. Although Gorbachev returned to power for a brief period, his grip had weakened and he resigned on August 24th, 1991. He was replaced by Boris Yeltsin in Russia's first free elections. The Communist Party officially disbanded after this and in December 1991, the USSR – along with the last remnants of the Cold War – broke up. Yeltsin declared that, 'The world can sigh again in relief'.

Differences and divides

As the years passed, many Germans became disheartened at how life in reunited Germany had turned out. In former East Germany, around two-thirds of all the senior public- and private-sector jobs were filled by people from the former West, and despite the billions of deutschmarks pumped into the former GDR, salaries remained much lower there than those in the west of the country. Many former West Germans shared this resentment as local, low-paid jobs tended to be filled by former East Germans willing to work for less money. 'Some people say it's a good thing, some people say we should build the Wall back up,' expressed one West German bricklayer, after seeing some of his business go to East Germans who had moved in and used government aid to undercut his prices.

Immigration
The new Germany was becoming a more appealing place to live. With borders being flung open all across Europe, the

GERMANY'S *new parliament*

In June 1991, the Bundestag began transferring parliament and government to Berlin. The new parliament and government were to be based in the Spreebogen, the area around the old Reichstag building, linking the eastern and western parts of Berlin. The Reichstag, the new seat of the German government, was given a new glass dome, and was opened to the public, givings visitors a bird's eye view of Germany's capital.

country was attracting more and more immigrants from Eastern Europe and beyond. Reunited Germany had no official immigration laws, so all immigrants had to do was enter as political refugees and hope the government would grant them asylum. By 1992, Germany was taking 78.8 per cent of all asylum seekers in Europe.

MURDER *in Molln*

On November 23rd, two neo-Nazis set fire to a Turkish family's house in a small town called Molln, killing a woman and two girls. The German public were revolted at this violence towards people who had been in Germany for several generations, and by the end of January 1993, nearly three million people had protested against the violence.

Neo-Nazis General unease at the number of people entering Germany exploded when it was announced in April 1991 that Poles would be allowed to enter Germany without visas. Neo-Nazis began blocking border-crossing points, and pelting Polish buses and cars. In June, 2,000 skinheads arrived in Dresden, shouting 'Heil Hitler!' and 'Auslander raus!' ('Foreigners out!'), giving Nazi salutes. During the summer of 1992, a number of disturbing attacks on immigrants and asylum seekers were reported in the German media. Germany's reputation suffered further when the courts treated these Neo-Nazi thugs leniently.

The Gulf War and Kosovo Not long after Germany had celebrated its unification, the first Gulf War began in January 1991. A pacifist Germany, still wary of military involvement, opted to offer financial support instead of sending troops. By the time the war was over, Germany had given around 5.3 billion marks to the war effort. However, just a few years later, Germany actively supported the NATO bombing campaign in Kosovo, and provided troops for the multinational force that entered the country in 1999.

The popularity of the Far Right soared in the reunited Germany. During 1992 alone, nearly 3,000 attacks on immigrants and other outsiders such as the homeless were recorded as West Germans grew increasingly resentful to supporting their neighbours in the old East Germany.

CLOSING *the past*

By the late 1990s, Germany had paid more than 104 billion marks in compensation to Hitler's victims. But after some high-profile business takeovers in Germany in 1998, Holocaust survivors in the USA filed a series of lawsuits against German companies who had used slave labourers during the war. In December 1999, Schroeder set up a 10 billion mark fund for the families of the former slave labourers.

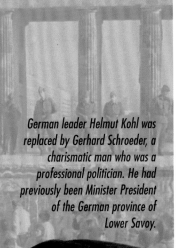

German leader Helmut Kohl was replaced by Gerhard Schroeder, a charismatic man who was a professional politician. He had previously been Minister President of the German province of Lower Savoy.

The European Union

After German reunification, Chancellor Kohl and French President Mitterrand began working on an ambitious project to bring Europe closer together. Kohl was determined that Germany should play a key role in this process. In December 1992, in Maastricht, Holland, a treaty was signed that committed 14 European nations to a stronger alliance. At another meeting in Holland in 1997, plans were announced for the launch of a single currency – the euro. Along with France, Germany was the major driving force behind integration. Kohl declared that 'the building of the United States of Europe' would be 'the major success story of the next century'.

Kohl voted out of office

On September 11th, 1998, Helmut Kohl – the driving force behind German reunification – was voted out of office. His popularity had slumped as many East Germans began to feel that he was not keeping his promises. Despite the fact that he had put aside billions of marks to revitalize the east of the country, many felt Kohl had not delivered the 'flourishing landscapes' he had promised them.

Schroeder's Germany

Kohl was replaced as Chancellor by the leader of the SPD, Gerhard Schroeder. A snappy dresser who liked to smoke expensive cigars, the new leader fired the imagination of the German public. Declaring that 'the era of Helmut Kohl is over', Schroeder promised a new era for Germany, together with wealth for all. He remained committed to the launch of the euro, but his attitude towards Germany's role in the world changed. Born in 1944, Schroeder was the first German chancellor who was too young to remember the war, and this had a major effect on his foreign policy.

Germany and European defence

Under Schroeder, Germany now began to take a more active role on the world stage. Around 4,000 armed German troops joined peacekeeping forces in Kosovo and Macedonia in 1999. Hoping that such participation might in some way make up for atrocities committed during World War II, Schroeder stated that 'German soldiers here are showing a Germany always hoped for in this region but not seen until now'. After this peacekeeper's role, Germany was also involved in successful operations to remove Afghanistan's Taliban regime in 2001.

Anniversary celebrations

On Tuesday, November 9th, 1999, Germany and most of the world stopped to remember the fall of the Wall ten years earlier. Former US President George Bush (Sr), the last Soviet leader Mikhail Gorbachev,

MEMORIAL *to the Wall*

In August 1998, plans were announced to erect a Wall memorial at the Bernauer Strasse. The monument was made up of a 70-metre piece of the Berlin Wall with slits cut into it and steel sheets at the end.

the German Chancellor Gerhard Schroeder and his predecessor Helmut Kohl arrived in Berlin for the occasion. In the streets musicians performed on the barren strip where the Wall used to stand and that once separated East from West. Children born as the Wall came down were also invited to come and celebrate their birthdays with Berlin's mayor.

The tenth anniversary celebrations drew tens of thousands of people to the centre of Berlin. Festivities included a New Year's Eve laser show by the Brandenburg Gate.

'The day will come when a German would not make an automatic apology every time they entered a room.'

Willy Brandt, former chancellor of West Germany, predicting a positive future for Germany.

The beginning of the 21st century has been an exciting time for Germany. More than ten years after the collapse of the Berlin Wall and the Soviet Bloc, Germany now has a new currency, the euro, and is at the centre of plans for a European army and an international criminal court. Many people in Germany are also hopeful that the gap will continue to narrow between residents of the former East and West. This would result in a truly united and content nation.

Hello euro

On January 1st, 2002, Germans replaced their deutschmarks with euros — the brand-new single currency of the European Union (EU). Germany has also continued to press for an enlargement of the European Union. By 2004, another ten nations will be admitted to the EU. In the future, Germany and its EU neighbours hope that the euro will become a serious rival to the US dollar, and will help create a more secure and prosperous Europe.

New terrors

Like many Western countries, the main threat to Germany is now coming not from traditional enemies but from terrorist organizations such as al-Qaeda. In the World Trade Center disaster on September 11th, 2001, many of the terrorists studied in Hamburg and formed illegal terrorist cells there. After this shocking event, Chancellor Gerhard Schroeder knew it was more urgent to support 'international alliances' against the 'privatized violence of... terrorists'.

Defence

In 2002, Germany – along with Holland – held the leadership of the International Security Assistance Force (ISAF) in Kabul, Afghanistan. But in 2003, along with France, Germany chose not to join an Anglo-American force that entered Iraq with the aim of destroying Saddam Hussein's dictatorship. Instead, they chose to support the force through increased aid to the United Nations.

Along with France, Germany was the driving force behind the single European currency, the euro. Despite teething problems, the currency eventually took off and Germany is the banking centre of the new Europe.

GERMANY *and the UN*

In 1996, the UN set up several organizations in Bonn, including the United Nations Information Centre. Then, on Janury 1st, 2003, Germany became a non-permanent member of the UN Security Council. Germany is also one of more than 60 states who have agreed to an International Criminal Court (ICC), which will see countries team up to make sure criminals are brought to justice.

A GIANT *economy*

Despite lean times at the beginning of the 21st century, Germany's economy remains powerful. It has an annual GDP worth over £1.25 trillion, and leads the world in producing chemicals, steel, machinery, vehicles and electronics. Many of the world's most famous car makers such as BMW, Mercedes and Porsche come from Germany. In fact, Germany stands second only to the United States in terms of world trade.

Germany is known for the quality of its manufacturing, particularly its cars. This exotic sports car (left) is made by the German firm BMW, who, along with Mercedes Benz, Porsche and Volkswagon, sell millions of cars all over the world each year.

European Army
Ever since countries started to group together in post-war Europe, there have been talks of a European Army. In 1991, France, Germany, Spain, Belgium and Luxembourg got together to create an armed force called Eurocorps, based in Strasbourg. This mini-army contained up to 60,000 troops and served in Bosnia-Herzegovina and Kosovo. However, Germany has stated that it wants to go much further than this and create a permanent European Army to replace national forces. Under the proposals for a rapid reaction force announced in 1999, a new EU force of up to 60,000 troops, with up to 400 combat aircraft will be created. It will be able to sustain an operation for up to a year.

Uniting people
One of the main problems facing Germany after reunification was the lack of equality between those living in the east and those in the west. To try to bring the two sides together, the government continues to pour huge sums of money into the former East Germany, investing in transportation and communication networks, as well stimulating job growth in small businesses. This massive investment is starting to show results. By 2000, manufacturers in eastern Germany were growing at a healthy rate, and many people think that by 2005, former East Germany will catch up with the rest of the country.

The Eurofighter Typhoon is a shining example of increasing European military co-operation. Four countries — Germany, Italy, Spain and Britain — are working together to produce fighter planes that can rival the top American models.

TIMELINE

1800–1938

- 1848: Publication of Marx and Engels' The Communist Manifesto. *It becomes very popular in parts of Europe, particularly Russia.*

- 1914: The assassination of Archduke Franz Ferdinand leads to the outbreak of World War I.

- 1917: Communist revolution topples czar in Russia.

- ▼ 1933: Hitler and his National Socialist (Nazi) Party are elected to power in Germany.

1939–1946

- 1939: Nazi-Soviet Pact, a non-aggression agreement, signed in August between Germany and the USSR.

- 1941: Hitler ignores the 1939 agreement with the USSR and his forces storm into the Soviet Union.

- December 7th, 1941: Japan launches an attack on Pearl Harbor, prompting the USA to enter World War II.

- 1945: World War II ends as the Allies defeat Hitler's troops.

- 1945: Yalta Conference held in February. The result of this is the dividing up of Germany and Berlin into regions controlled by the four Allied powers.

- 1945: Agreement formulated at Potsdam between July 17th–August 2nd, making Germany pay for its actions during the war.

- 1946: Sir Winston Churchill makes 'Iron Curtain' speech, declaring that 'an iron curtain has descended across the continent' in response to the conversion to communism of Poland, Hungary and Czechoslovakia.

1947–1952

- 1947: Truman Doctrine announced in March, followed by the Marshall Plan in June.

- 1948: Berlin Blockade and Airlift begin in June. Over one million tons of supplies are delivered to the ctiy, including a gift of a camel called Clarence!

- 1948: USSR explode their first nuclear bomb.

- 1949: USA, Canada and several European nations form NATO (North Atlantic Treat Organization) as well as the official formation of the GDR (German Democratic Republic) in East Germany and the FRG (Federal Republic of Germany) in West Germany.

- 1949: Mao Tse-tung founds the communist People's Republic of China on October 1st.

1953–1960

- 1953: Stalin dies in the USSR, aged 74.

- 1955: Warsaw Pact formed. It was a military alliance of the Eastern European Soviet Bloc countries set up in response to the NATO alliance. Its members were the Soviet Union, Albania, Bulgaria, Romania, East Germany, Hungary, Poland, and Czechoslovakia — all the communist countries of Eastern Europe except Yugoslavia.

- 1955: War begins in Vietnam between the US-supported Republic of Vietnam in the South and the Communist Democratic Republic of Vietnam in the North.

- 1956: November uprising in Hungary is brutally crushed by the Soviet army.

1961–1970

1971–1988

1989–1990

1991–2004

▲ *1961: Construction of Berlin Wall begins during the night of Sunday, August 13th.*

• *1962: Cuban Missile Crisis in October. The world comes close to war as Kennedy and Krushchev fall out over USSR missiles stationed in Cuba. The Soviet leader eventually agrees to remove the missiles.*

• *1963: Kennedy visits the Berlin Wall on June 26th, 1963 and makes his famous 'Ich Bin Ein Berliner' speech.*

• *1968: Beginning of Prague Spring in Czechoslovakia. The reformist leader, Dubcek, is removed when Soviet troops invade the country.*

• *1970: Ostpolitik agreement announced by Chancellor Brandt of West Germany. The FRG and GDR exchange ambassadors for the first time.*

• *1973: USA admits defeat in Vietnam and the entire Asian country becomes communist in 1975.*

• *1979: Soviet Union invades Afghanistan. The USA immediately abandons promises made at the SALT conferences in response.*

• *1981: Ronald Reagan elected President of USA.*

• *1985: Gorbachev elected leader of USSR.*

• *June 1989: Communists lose election in Poland.*

• *October 1989: Gorbachev visits Berlin and comes face-to-face with protestors appealing to him for help.*

• *November 1989: Berlin Wall falls on the evening of November 9th.*

• *December 1989: Communist government dissolves in Czechoslovakia and an uprising in Romania topples the hated dictator Ceausescu. Free elections are also announced in Hungary.*

• *April 1990: Free elections lead to non-communist government in Bulgaria.*

• *1990: East and West Germany reunited on October 3rd.*

• *1991: Gorbachev removed from power in USSR by coup. He is reinstated after protests led by Boris Yelstin, but later replaced by the latter. The Communist Party in USSR resigns and dissolves itself.*

• *1991: Start of the first Gulf War. Germany commits financial aid rather than troops.*

• *1991: New parliament to be built in Berlin.*

• *1991: Maastricht treaty signed.*

• *1998: Kohl replaced as German leader by Schroeder.*

• *1999: Germany commits troops to Kosovo.*

• *1999: Germany signs up to single European currency, linking the deutschmark to the euro on January 1st.*

• *1999: The renovated Reichstag, home to Germany's new parliament, opens on April 19th.*

• *2002: Euro replaces deutschmark in Germany.*

• *2003: Start of second Gulf War. Germany opts out.*

• *2004: EU welcomes Czech Republic, Cyprus, Estonia, Hungary, Latvia, Lithuania, Malta, Poland, Slovakia, Slovenia.*

GLOSSARY

airlift The delivery of goods and essential supplies by aircraft. The Berlin Airlift took place in 1948 after the Soviets imposed a blockade in West Berlin, starving it of supplies.

Allies Friendly countries who join together to face a problem. In World War II, the Allies included the USA, Britain and the Commonwealth, the USSR and France who joined together to fight the Axis forces of Germany, Japan and Italy.

asylum seeker A person who flees from persecution or trouble in one country and tries to stay in another country for their own safety.

Cold War The period after World War II which describes the tension between the communist countries (led by the USSR) and the capitalist west (led by the United States). There was no direct confrontation during this period, but the political rivalry between the two groups was very intense.

capitalist A person who believes in the importance of individual rights and the ability of a person to create their own financial rewards, with as little interference from governments as possible.

chancellor The title of Germany's leader.

checkpoint A post on a boundary or border where a person's identification papers are checked as they pass from one region to another.

communist A person who believes in the paramount importance of society over the individual. In a communist society, all property is owned by the state, with everyone sharing in the nation's wealth.

democratic A system of government where all of a country's population has a vote in choosing who runs that nation's government.

deutschmark The old German currency.

emigration The movement of people out of one region or country.

euro The single European currency which replaced the old currencies in many European countries, including Germany, France, Ireland, Holland and Spain.

FRG Federal Republic of Germany, the official title of West Germany. The FRG was created in1949 by the merger of the three areas of Germany that had been controlled by Britain, the USA and France after World War II.

GDP Gross Domestic Product. This is a measure of the amount of money that an entire country produces each year from all aspects of business and industry.

GDR German Democratic Republic, the official name for East Germany. The GDR was created in 1949 from the area of Germany controlled by Soviet forces after the end of World War II.

graffiti Drawings or words, written or painted on a wall.

Gulf Wars The two conflicts that occurred in 1991 and 2003 in which a coalition of forces, led by the USA, fought against Iraqi forces under the leadership of Saddam Hussein. The first Gulf War was in response to Iraq's invasion of Kuwait. The second Gulf War saw the removal from power of Saddam Hussein.

Holocaust The term used to describe the genocide of the Nazi regime during World War II in which millions of Jews, eastern Europeans and gypsies were sent to concentration camps and killed.

immigration The movement of people into a region or country.

Iron Curtain The term used to describe the dividing line in Europe between capitalist countries in the West and communist countries in the East. It was first used by Winston Churchill in 1946.

mujahedeen The term used to describe Afghan Islamic fighters who fought a guerrilla war against Soviet forces who invaded Afghanistan in 1979.

NATO North Atlantic Treaty Organization. A coalition of Western countries, including Britain, the USA, France and Canada, in response to the apparent threat from communist countries.

Nazi Short for National Socialist, this term describes a person with extreme fascist political views who rose to power in Germany in the 1930s under the leadership of Adolf Hitler.

Neo-Nazi A term used to describe somebody today who believes in the political views of the Nazis.

newsflash A short and unexpected news bulletin which reveals a story that is just breaking.

Ostpolitik A policy developed by Willy Brandt who was German chancellor in the 1960s and 1970s. It tried to improve political relations between West Germany and its communist neighbours.

peacekeeping force A military force that is sent into a war-torn region in an attempt to keep the peace.

propaganda The manipulation of information and news so that a particular political message can by conveyed.

reunification The joining together of something that used to be unified. Germany was split into two countries, the FRG and GDR, after World War II and these were reunified in 1990.

SALT Strategic Arms Limitation Talks. A series of meetings between the political leaders of the USA and USSR in which the limiting of nuclear weapons was discussed and several important agreements were made.

SDI Strategic Defence Initiative. Also called 'Star Wars', this was a high-tech defence system developed by the USA which was supposed to destroy incoming Soviet nuclear missiles.

shoot-to-kill The decision to shoot someone with the intention of killing them rather than just hurting them.

soviet The name of a council in a communist country. The term was also used to describe anything or anyone from one of the former communist countries.

Soviet Bloc The name given to the communist countries of Eastern Europe (also called Eastern Bloc).

Stasi The secret police of the GDR. They were responsible for collecting information on people inside their own country and were also guilty of kidnappings, brutality and torture.

Taliban An extreme Islamic group who seized power in Afghanistan and imposed a strict Muslim regime on the country. The Taliban were toppled from power when American-led forces invaded the country in 2002.

trade union A group which represents workers from a particular industry and negotiates on their behalf on issues such as wages and work conditions.

USSR Union of Soviet Socialist Republics. The enormous communist country which was formed by the unification of several regions, including Russia, Latvia, the Ukraine and Georgia. The USSR broke up in 1991 after the removal of the Communist Party from power.

vote-rigging The fixing of an election result by doctoring the votes.

Warsaw Pact The coalition of former communist countries, including the USSR, Poland, East Germany and Czechoslovakia, in response to the foundation of NATO by Western countries.

INDEX

A

Adenauer, Konrad 13
Afghanistan 18, 39, 40, 43, 45
Aktuelle Kamera 24
Albania 42
Alliance for Germany Party 34
al-Qaeda 40
anniversaries 39
ARD 24, 26
Associated Press 22
asylum seekers 37, 44
Attlee, Clement 4
Austria 20

B

Basic Treaty 18
Belgium 41
Berlin 6, 8, 10, 11, 12, 13, 14,
    15, 16, 21, 22, 23, 28, 29,
    30, 34, 35, 36, 39, 42, 43
    Airlift 13, 42, 44
    Blockade 12, 13, 42
    Control Council 12
    East 5, 11, 14, 15, 20, 21,
    27, 33
    West 5, 11, 12, 13, 14, 15,
    19, 20, 21, 22, 25, 26, 27,
    29, 30, 32, 44
Bernauer Strasse 16, 39
BMW 41
Bonn 35, 40
Bornholmer Strasse 23, 24, 25,
    27, 28
Bosnia-Herzegovina 41
Brandenburg Gate 15, 19,
    28, 29, 39
Brandt, Willy 17, 39
Britain 4, 9, 10, 11, 13, 15,
    32, 41, 44, 45

Budapest 20
Bulgaria 17, 42, 43
Bundestag 36
bunkers 16
Bush, George (Sr) 33, 39

C

Canada 11, 42, 45
capitalism 8
Castro, Fidel 17
Ceausescu, Elena 31
Ceausescu, Nicolae 31, 43
checkpoints 4, 15, 16, 22, 23,
    27, 44
Checkpoint Charlie
    (Friedrichstrasse) 4, 15, 17,
    19, 21, 24, 25, 26, 27,
    28, 34
China 42
Churchill, Winston 12, 42, 45
Cold War 7, 17, 18, 19,
    36, 44
communism 8, 9, 12, 18,
    31, 42
Communist Manifesto, The 8,
    42
Council of Europe 12
coups 36, 43
Cuba 16, 43
Cyprus 43
czars 8, 42
Czechoslovakia 7, 9, 11, 17,
    18, 20, 22, 31, 42, 43
Czech Republic 43

D

deutschmarks 13, 30, 32, 35,
    38, 40, 43, 44
Dixon, Ursula Grosser 35

Dreilinden 15
Dresden 30, 37
Dubcek, Alexander 17, 31, 43

E

Engels, Friedrich 8, 42
Estonia 43
Eurofighter Typhoon 41
euro 7, 38, 40, 43, 44
European Army 41
European Coal and Steel
    Community 12
European Union 12, 40, 41

F

Fechter, Peter 16
France 4, 10, 11, 13, 15, 32,
    38, 41, 44, 45
Ferdinand, Archduke Franz 42
FRG (Federal Republic of
    Germany) 4, 10, 13, 17,
    19, 20, 22, 32, 42, 43, 44

G

Germany 4, 7, 8, 9, 10, 20,
    32, 34, 35, 36, 37, 38, 40,
    41, 42, 43, 44, 45
    reunification 19, 29, 32,
    34, 35, 37, 38, 43, 45
GDR (German Democratic
    Republic) 6, 10, 13, 15,
    17, 21, 22, 23, 24, 28, 36,
    42, 43, 44, 45
Glasnost 19
Godek, Major Bernie 26
Gorbachev, Mikhail 6, 16, 18,
    19, 21, 30, 33, 36, 39, 43
Gorbachev, Raisa 19
graffiti 19, 44

Greis-Behrendt, Erdmute 23
Gueffroy, Chris 20, 35
gulags 8
Gulf Wars 37, 43, 44

H

Hamburg 40
Heinrich-Heine-Strasse 27
Helmstedt 15
Helsinki Accord 18
Herman, Ken 13
Hitler, Adolf 4, 9, 10, 37, 38,
    42, 45
Holocaust 38, 44
Holland 38, 40
Honecker, Erich 14, 18, 19, 20,
    21, 35
Honecker, Margot 21
Hungary 12, 17, 18, 20,
    31, 42, 43
Hussein, Saddam 40

I

immigration 37
inflation 9
International Criminal
    Court 40
Iraq 40
Iron Curtain 11, 12, 42, 45
ISAF (International Security
    Assistance Force) 40
Italy 12, 41, 44

J

Jaeger, Harald 23, 25, 27
Jaruzelski, General 20
Jews 9, 44
John Paul II, Pope 21
journalists 22, 23

K

Kabul 40
Kennedy, John F 14, 17, 43
Khalou, Thomas 23
Kohl, Helmut 19, 30, 32,
    33, 35, 37, 38, 39, 43
Kosovo 37, 39, 41, 43
Kremlin 14
Krenz, Egon 21, 22, 35
Krushchev, Nikita 12, 13, 14,
    17, 43

L

Lanser, Bernard 16
Latvia 43
Leipzig 20, 33
Leninplatz 34
Lenin, Vladimir 8, 34
Lithuania 43
loans 18
Luxembourg 41

M

Marienfelde 14
Maastricht 38, 43
Macedonia 39
Malta 43
Mao Tse-tung 42
Marshall Plan 12, 42
Marx, Karl 8, 42
Mazowiecki, Tadeusz 21
memorials 39
Mercedes 41
Middle East 36
Mitterrand, Francois 19,
    32, 37
Modrow, Hans 30, 31, 33, 34
Molln 37
Moscow 18, 33

N

Nagy, Prime Minister 12
NATO (North Atlantic Treaty
    Organization) 11, 12, 35,
    37, 42, 45
Nazis 10, 42, 45
Nazi-Soviet Pact 10, 42
Neo-Nazis 36, 37, 45
newspapers 11, 20
nuclear missiles 17, 18, 43, 45

O

Olympic Games 18
Ostpolitik 17, 43, 45

P

Pearl Harbor 42
Perestroika 19
pilots 13
Poland 9, 11, 17, 20, 21, 31,
    42, 43
Porsche 41
Porter, Henry 28
Potsdam Agreement 10, 42
Potsdamer Platz 29
Prague 16, 17, 20, 22, 31
    Prague Spring 17, 43
propaganda 10, 11, 45
Pterck, Rainer 24

R

Reagan, Ronald 16, 18, 19, 43
Red Terror 8
Reichstag 36, 43
reparations 9, 10, 42
Reuters 22
Romania 31, 42, 43
Rudower Chaussee 27
Russian Revolution 8

Ryl, Torsten 26

S

SALT (Strategic Arms Limitation
    Talks) 18, 43, 45
S-Bahn 14, 15
Schabowski, Gunter 22, 23,
    24, 35
Schroeder, Gerhard 38, 39,
    40, 43
Schwarker, Jurgen 26
SDI (Strategic Defence
Initiative)
    18, 45
slave labourers 38
Slovakia 43
Slovenia 43
Solidarity 21, 30
Spain 41
Spreebogen 36
Stalin, Joseph 4, 8, 10, 11,
    12, 13, 42
Stasi 32, 33, 45
Strasbourg 41

T

Taliban 39, 45
terrorists 40
Thatcher, Margaret 32
Toft, Chris 28
Trabants 30, 32
Truman Doctrine 12, 42
Truman, Harry 4, 12, 13
Two Plus Four Treaty 35

U

Ukraine 11
Ulbricht, Walter 14
United Nations 40

Security Council 40
United Nations Information
    Centre 40
Urban, Rudolf 16
USA 4, 10, 11, 12, 13, 15,
    17, 18, 33, 38, 41, 42, 43,
    44, 45
USSR 4, 5, 6, 7, 8, 10, 11, 12,
    13, 18, 33, 36, 42, 43, 44,
    45

V

Vienna 14
Vietnam 16, 18, 42, 43
Voigt, Bill 13
Volkswagen 38, 41
vote-rigging 20, 45

W

Wache, Angela 26
Walesa, Lech 31
Warsaw 30
Warsaw Pact 11, 12, 42, 45
watchtowers 15, 16
West Berlin Philharmonic
    Orchestra 29
World Trade Center 40
World War I 9, 42
World War II 4, 8, 9, 10, 35,
    39, 42, 44

Y

Yalta 10, 42
Yeltsin, Boris 36, 43
Yugoslavia 42

Z

ZDF 24
Zimmerstrasse 16

ACKNOWLEDGEMENTS

Copyright © ticktock Entertainment Ltd 2003
First published in Great Britain in 2003 by ticktock Media Ltd.,
Unit 2, Orchard Business Centre, North Farm Road, Tunbridge Wells, Kent, TN2 3XF

ISBN 1 86007 422 7 pbk
ISBN 1 86007 429 4 hbk
Printed in Taiwan

A CIP catalogue record for this book is available from the British Library.

We would like to thank: Tall Tree Ltd, Lizzy Bacon and Ed Simkins for their assistance.

10 9 8 7 6 5 4 3 2 1

Picture Credits
Every effort has been made to trace the copyright holders, and we apologize in advance for any unintentional omissions.
We would be pleased to insert the appropriate acknowledgements in any subsequent edition of this publication.

B = bottom; C = centre; L = left; R = right; T = top.
Alamy: 9b & 42b. Corbis: 1c, 4t & b, 5t, 7t, 8t, 11c, 12b, 13b, 15t, 16t, 17b, 18t, 19b, 21t, 26b, 28t, 29t & b, 30t, 31b, 32b, 36b, 37b, 39b, 42c, Hulton Archive:
14b & 43t. 21b, 25b, PA Photos: 22t & b, 24b, 25b.